TSIGAN:
The Gypsy Poem

(new edition)

Cecilia Woloch

Two Sylvias Press

Copyright © 2018 Cecilia Woloch

All rights reserved. No part of this book may be reproduced in any form without the written permission of the publisher, except for brief quotations embodied in critical articles and reviews.

Two Sylvias Press
PO Box 1524
Kingston, WA 98346
twosylviaspress@gmail.com

Cover Artist: Jonde Northcutt
Cover Design: Kelli Russell Agodon
Book Design: Annette Spaulding-Convy
Author Photo: Mark Savage

Created with the belief that *great writing is good for the world*, Two Sylvias Press mixes modern technology, classic style, and literary intellect with an eco-friendly heart. We draw our inspiration from the poetic literary talent of Sylvia Plath and the editorial business sense of Sylvia Beach. We are an independent press dedicated to publishing the exceptional voices of writers.

For more information about Two Sylvias Press please visit:
www.twosylviaspress.com

For more information and press materials about *Tsigan* please visit:
www.ceciliawoloch.com

Second Edition. Created in the United States of America.
First Edition published by Cahuenga Press, 2001

ISBN- 978-0-9986314-7-9

Two Sylvias Press
www.twosylviaspress.com

Table of Contents

Author's Note (First Edition)

Section I   / 1

Section II   / 45

Section III: Coda   / 107

Author's Note (Second Edition)   / 123

Acknowledgements   / 133

Author   / 139

Author's Note (First Edition)

For as long as I can remember, it's been a kind of running joke in my family: that our wildness might be explained by "Gypsy blood" on our father's side. As is the case for so many children and grandchildren of immigrants, our lost history has been a source of fascination for us — for all of my brothers and sisters, but especially, it seems, for me — made all the more fascinating by the reluctance or inability of our elders to elucidate certain mysteries.

I never knew my paternal grandmother except through the stories I heard — and sometimes overheard — about her. Probably, as all eavesdroppers do, I distorted some things; certainly imagination has filled in gaps in those stories, too. And because she died before I was born — in fact, seemed to have vanished without leaving a trace, as had the second of her husbands, my father's father, who died before my father was born — this grandmother, who was notorious for her wanderlust and for "reading the cards," who was lovingly but also rather darkly referred to as "Tsiganka," or "little Gypsy," became something of a myth for me, and something of a muse. It's possible that the sobriquet only applied to her metaphorically, but as W.S. Merwin, in his poem, "Gift," insists, "I have to trust what was given to me/if I am to trust anything ... I must be led by what was given to me."

So I allowed this fascination, and my own wanderlust, to lead me all the way back to the village where my grandmother was born, on a series of journeys that took place over the course of a number of years. Along the way, what I learned about the actual Gypsies, the Roma people — about their culture and history and how they're perceived by many Europeans, a perception so different from the romanticized, even glamorous image we have of Gypsies in the U.S. — helped me to understand why my older relatives were always so secretive about the possibility of "Gypsy blood."

Ultimately, many of those family mysteries remain mysteries; and the Gypsies' history, like the history of my family, remains shadowy. But in the search for the source of my own restlessness, my own sense of exile and otherness, I stumbled into a kind of communion with the world — which is, in any case, never still — and I have to believe there's grace in that, and luck.

Cecilia Woloch, 2001

TSIGAN:
The Gypsy Poem

for my sisters and brothers

"[I visited] a camp of Gypsies at Rouen... they excite the hatred of the bourgeois even though inoffensive as sheep. This hatred is linked to something very deep and complex. It is found in all orderly people. It is the hatred that they feel for the bedouin, the heretic, the philosopher, the solitary, the poet. And there is fear in that hatred."

(Gustav Flaubert, in a letter to George Sand, ca. 1865)

I

Oh little shadow. Little lurker into doorways. Little Gypsy Gypsy Gypsy of a girl. Whose bird you were. Whose darkling in the branches on the underside of morning thrashed them shimmering with parting as I turned. Who disappeared. Each bitter word or look dropped like a coin into your pocket, small gold hidden in the blind folds of your skirt. Keep back. Come close. In cities made of falling and not falling, smell of smoke. Smell of wind and blood and ashes. Smell of dancing and of soot. They say a Gypsy blacksmith forged the nails to kill their Christ; that's the reason someone set the church bells ringing, sky in flames. And when you ran — burned from the clearing, all those black wings beating, beating — who ran with you, just behind you or before you, also flew? So spit your luck into the embers. Flash your name, if that's your jewel. What cannot be torn away from you is deeper fire: sing.

1192: India — Battle of Terain. Last Roma (also known as "Gypsies") leave India for the West.

1347: Byzantium — Black death reaches Constantinople. Roma move west again.

1385: Romania — First recorded transaction of Gypsy slaves.

That Gypsy blood —
my mother laughed
(I was so young,
so dark myself:
slant-eyed and sulking
in my *teta's* kitchen,
feeding god my crusts.)
It was a joke, I thought,
a secret overheard,
whispered through smoke —
The walls have ears,
my mother sighed,
but teta's fists flew from her hips,
she waved her hands
like startled birds
and warned them, *No —*
whose shadows danced between us—
Tell me, I thought,
Tell.

1416: Germany — First anti-Romani law is issued, accusing Gypsies of being *foreign spies, carriers of the plague, and traitors to Christendom.*

Crones: I didn't know
this word for *old,
fierce women, hags* —
I called them *teta*
*(Teta Sue, Aunt
Teta Annie)*
for the clicking
of their tongues
against their teeth,
the way they danced
the polka — flying,
spinning, cackling —
how they hissed,
whispered to me
(Eat, honey, eat) —
their kitchens dim
with steam and Jesus
on the wall above us
— lamb-eyed, heart
like meat — for how
they crossed themselves
and spit and tried
to fatten me with sweets
*(poor thing, poor thing —
the sickly daughter
of their own

dead sister's son)
who were my great-aunts,
Daddy's aunts —
one who'd hushed
strange men in her attic,
one who'd stashed
the bathtub gin,
once found my father
as a small boy stuffing
grass into his mouth
and promised: *this one
will be fed* —
I called them *teta*
for his sake
and for the secrets
that they kept —
where we'd come from,
what was hidden
in their apron pockets, what
could not be claimed —
their laughter rising up
like crows, black-
winged, their hands
waving me back — *Don't
ask, don't ask* — and for
the wild and ancient music
of such names.

1418: France — First Gypsies reported in Colmar.

1419: Belgium — First Gypsies reported in Antwerp.

1420: Holland — First Gypsies reported in Deventer.

What I was told:

*Your grandmother bought herself
a big black car and disappeared.
Wore black hats cocked
across one eye. Didn't tell no one
where she went.*

Maybe down to Atlantic City to gamble?
(God is luck.)

What I was not told:
How she died.

What I was not supposed to hear:
One rumor — *suicide.*
One rumor — *that last husband
murdered her, then vanished, too.*

One teta sighs; one shakes her head.
No one wants to remember, honey.

*I don't have no picture
of your grandfather. I don't
have no photograph.*

My grandmother
who never was
my grandmother,
who stopped the clock
by throwing up her hands,
whose name was lost
among the names
of men she married,
who forgot
to think ahead into my life,
to live to tell me
how she read the cards,
prepared the dead
for burial, the living
to give birth —

who was mortician,
midwife,
barber
in that village
in the old country;
a bride at thirteen, sold
to an old man
whom she fled —

made her way
across the ocean
to America — but how? —
married again
(this time for love?)

a man who sang,
whose name was *Vloch*
(a Vlach? Wallachian?)
then *Woloch* —
at its root, the word
for *stranger*
everywhere—
and made his name
her name —

made bathtub gin
out of potato peels,
made lace
of bitten threads;
made *her mark* —
an *X* across
the coroner's report
that said the death
of *Harry Woloch* —
who would have been
my grandfather —
was not the fault

of the cop whose bullets
struck him in the back —
below: *or so
I have been told* —

who was a widow,
twenty-nine and two weeks
pregnant, so she wed
the miner, widower,
the drunk
who tried to suffocate
the child (who would become
the man, my father —
not his son —)
whose shack she swept
and whom she cut her hair
to spite —

who lost three sons
as little boys
(a daughter stillborn?)
a grown son *gone
to soldier*, killed
by Nazis in the last
days of the war —

who fled again,
who disappeared,
who was a witch,
a *Red*, a Communist —
her last two sons
in prison (one my father
— for what crimes?) —

who reappeared,
married again —
that final husband,
all we know of him:
a Russian — murderer?
Or was it suicide —
which god
(a pill or blade)
lay in her palm?
Or was it only
her bad heart?

Whose name was *Mary*,
also *Marya, Marushka,*
as in: *dear.*
Who was called *Tsiganka,*
Gypsy, as in: *she*
who vanishes.

1498: Germany (Holy Roman Empire) — Expulsion of Gypsies ordered.

1547: England — Death penalty imposed for any Gypsy not leaving the country within a month.

1637: Sweden — Death penalty for Gypsies not leaving the country.

1721: Austro-Hungarian Empire — Emperor Karl VI orders the extermination of Roma ("Gypsies") throughout his domain.

1728: Holland — Last Roma hunted down.

We are this line on a map
and this
and this invisible line
my father traced
with one thick finger: *this
is where we come from*
he would say:
the Carpathians—

nothing there
beneath his hand but paper
nothing there
that hasn't been erased
redrawn
dreamt of.

In that neighborhood of new-born trees,
of tender grass and cloud,
we were the wildest, loudest ones;
we were too many for our house.
You shouldn't let those kids climb on your car!
the neighbors warned.
Their car, our father called across the lawns —
belongs to *them*.
Our mother singing at the kitchen window,
watching birds build nests.

You lived like Gypsies, someone says
when I say, *This is how we lived:*
we slept entwined,
some nights climbed out
our bedroom windows to the roof
or dragged our blankets to the yard,
slung sheets from branches, made our tents.

Horreur du domecil — how Baudelaire
described this fear — Suburbia: the hush
of each door locked; the sky nailed shut.

Once *migrant, immigrant* —
we tore those roots
out of the ground,
moved further south —
left Pennsylvania (where the mills
were shutting down, the mines
long gone) for five wild
acres in Kentucky, lush
with fescue, pitched our camp
then built a house
(*with our own hands*)
dug in, took root,
flowered again —

(though I would always be the one branch —
wind-bent, reaching
reaching back —)

And in those rooms our father built
among the trees we perched like birds —
well, we could always fly again,
have always flown.

Our father's stories: how his family fled
each tenement by night —
before the landlord's wanting rent
(before the beating at the door) —

and in the next place any warmth
came from their gathering in it.
(*Gypsies at their fire in the yard,
the doors ajar*).

Summer: Daddy crouching on his haunches
tends the sparks.
The house is empty: we are here.
The house he always builds and builds.
And we are burning up the wood leftover —
laughing, eating ash.

We know exactly where we live.
He moves the smoke; he waves one hand.

1802: France — Roma in Basque province rounded up and imprisoned.

1812: Finland — Order to confine nomadic Gypsies in workhouses.

1830: Germany — Authorities in Nordhausen remove Roma children from their families for fostering with non-Roma.

1835: Denmark —Travelers hunted down in Jutland.

Daddy called me *Tsiganka*
when I began to wander
restlessly the world.
Just like your grandmother, he'd say
and touch my hair
(*the Kushner hair*)
and kiss my forehead
(where the priest had once left ash)
as if to mark me:
you will never be afraid
to not stand still;
as if to bless me
where I stood,
where I would stand:
you will not kneel.

1856: Romania — Emancipation of Gypsy slaves in Wallachia.

Simply to fly, to turn
on wind, on whim, set off
begin again —
new world
old world
new world
and this:
girl with a suitcase
(rushing where?)
woman alone, mid-air
a language in her hands
(unwritten still) —
bird of a chance
bird of a chance
carried toward what carries her.

> "It was a past that changed gradually as he advanced on his journey, because the traveler's past changes according to the route he has followed ..."
> — Italo Calvino, <u>Invisible Cities</u>

I wander through Paris reading a book called *Bury Me Standing* wherever I go. I read in the metro, read in cafés, read in the beautiful palace gardens drenched in wind and winter sun. I sit in the Tuilleries *filling my head* (as my mother would say) with the stories and facts. Gypsies traded as slaves in Romania hundreds of years ago. Gypsies burned out of their camps all over Eastern Europe now. Gypsies who lurk at the stations and borders, trading their luck for worse luck, worse and worse. Gypsies as in *Egyptians*, who came first from India, perhaps. Who mixed with the poor of Wallachia (ghost of my father's father's name): *"Not so much nomadic by nature, as that they were never allowed to stay."*

I look up from these words at the Eiffel Tower, think: *We have no monuments.* No white-eyed statues of gods and goddesses (*the only god is luck.*). Children are sailing toy boats in the fountain; empires are rising and falling again. And where is my place in all of this? Which terrible history is mine?

Well, nothing belongs to me, least of all memory; even the past keeps transforming, the dead. Even the image I've kept of the uncle I loved best begins to shift. Dark prince with his one gold tooth; black sheep with his pockets full of cash. As if he is coming toward me again in this wind, saying, *Now that you understand nothing, you can begin to understand.* Whispering, *Princess*, from his deathbed in the ward for indigents, *When I get out of here, I'm going to tell you something ...* Then he's gone. Then only movement, the stirring of shadows. The leaves of the trees are turning from green to silver, flashing like coins in the sun.

☙

Black sheep, that uncle went
from one reform school to the next
and from reform school into prison
and from prison, straight to war —
lied his way to France and back;
changed his name to "fox" — *Renard* —
brought us every summer some new aunt
—shimmering, blonde —oh women
loved the way his one gold tooth
shot light into his smile, that flashy
Cadillac, his eyes bright Slavic blue,
his skin as bronze as an Egyptian's;
how he softly spoke their names
like folded money —*Gypsy, outlaw* —
how he kept from being caught until
the sweet of rot set in — *gangrene*,
they said they'd amputate the leg —
When I get out of here, he whispered,
made one final dark escape.

1928: Germany — Nomadic Roma to be placed under permanent police surveillance.

A small boy on the rue de Sevigny
clings to his mother as I pass.
She hisses, "*Où, où est la sorcière ?*" —
asking him, "*Where,
where is the witch?*"

My long coat trailing in the wind,
my dark hair flying, wild, unkempt.
How do they know me,
the little ones?

(What is the bitterest name
you have ever been called?
Don't come near —
ne me touchez pas.)

1939: Germany — Gypsy fortunetellers arrested and sent to Ravensbruck concentration camp.

1940: France — French government opens internment camps for nomads.

Beware of them—
warned everywhere against
those women wearing
cardboard signs on strings
around their necks:

They'll use the signs
to hide their hands
and rob you blind—
Gypsy as thief.

Gypsy as woman dressed in black
and blackbird quick.
Gypsy as Witch.

In Rome, first feral cats
creep through the coliseum
wild-eyed
then the moon.

Morning in Madrid
(having been all night
on the train from Barcelona
jarred awake)
the first café:
all smoke and sunlight
sipping coffee, 9 a.m.
among the workingmen
who lean against the counter
businessmen:
a small boy enters
walks from man to man
to beg
is waved away
then stands in front of me
hands cupped
all eyes
have turned
in silence, watch:
he lifts his small dark face
to mine
his small hands
near enough
to touch, and held
between us

— knife-sharp, bright —
a chance
I recognize too late
(a flash of wings
against my ribs —
don't look at him)
I shake my head —

the silence shatters
(laughter, coins)
he turns and runs
into the street
into the din
of traffic, bells —
I turn and rush
to follow him:
he's swift and thin
he's just a boy
my nephew's age
(seven or eight)
and with his face
(a face I love) —
what name to call
to call him back
what language —*stop!*
I'm sorry, wait, come here—
pesetas in my palm?

And do I catch the boy
or not? Do I touch
his slender shoulder
till he faces me again:
push damp bills
into his hands
(all that I have —
is that enough?)

or stand there
sobbing in the crush
of strangers, laughter
at my back?

Everywhere in Spain
men and women crouch
in doorways, hold
limp children in their arms —
are they simply
sleeping, simply slack
with hunger —
dead?

Don't give those Gypsies anything.
Where there is one
there are a hundred
more than you could ever feed.

How then to eat?
How then to breathe?
How then to beat back
what keeps rising in me —
black-winged
sinned against?

1940: Germany/Lands Under German Occupation — *January*: The first genocidal action of the Holocaust takes place in Buchenwald, when 250 Romani children are used as guinea-pigs to test the Zyklon-B gas crystals.

In Warsaw, blackbird girls
swoop down in flocks
the old town square a swirl
of dark-eyed dark-haired girls
in brilliant skirts who circle
trilling at my waist
throw up their arms
to beg for sweets
who know among the tourists
whom to choose
(how do they know?)
so being chosen, being glad
in any language (*tak*
means *yes*)
I let them pick from sticky cakes
behind the glass, the old proprietress
glares back at me
and thinks, *Amerykanka, idiotka*
but cannot refuse
my cash (how far
in zlotys dollars go!)
so I buy cake for every girl
then watch them fly away again
their small hands sugared, glittering
as if I'd given
jewels to them
the sky above the bitter city
sharp as diamonds then.

"Gypsies were incarcerated with Jews in the ghettoes of Bialystok, Krakow, Lodz, L'viv, Radom and Warsaw. …The total number of Gypsies brought into [one] ghetto was eleven dead and 4,996 living. Of those, 2,686 were children."

>   — Isabel Fonseca, <u>Bury Me Standing: The Gypsies and Their Journey</u>

She'll have come to the church in Lodz to beg. A woman not older than I am and not more poorly-dressed — blue jeans, a jacket, her face scrubbed clean. Still, she'll stand with her palm upturned in front of the heavy wooden doors, so we'll have to step past her, as if she's not there, as if to step through her, invisible. My young friend muttering something in Polish I'm not meant to understand.

We'll have come to the church in Lodz to gaze at the face of the Black Madonna — *Our Mother of the Bright Mountain, Our Mother of the Sharp Gates.* The dark icon looming above the altar, her cheek marked with two jagged slashes, as if by the passage from girlhood to motherhood, the passage through innocence. A flutter like wings in her womb, I'll imagine; the angel saying, *Be not afraid.*

Or the kind of scars barbed wire would make.

There had been a Jew in the camp at Lodz, a doctor made to dig Jewish graves, who remembered the music that came from the Gypsy side, over the *Zigeunerlager* wall — the sounds of violins and guitars — and how, one day, abruptly, the music stopped. Then silence, *broken only by the screams of the tortured ... and the bellows of their executioners*. Only the Jewish doctor, Abram Rosenberg, would live to tell of this: *I discovered that every day the kripo came to the camp and ordered the Gypsies to hang their nearest and dearest. Their own children. Their kith and kin.*

In the church in Lodz, the woman will kneel in a narrow aisle between rows of pews. Back straight, hands clasped at her chest; eyes fixed on the scarred Madonna's face. A priest will walk quietly over the cold stone floor and remove her — though gently, *remove*. Taking her arm by the elbow and lifting, then guiding her swiftly away.

Out in the streets, there will be cafés, fountains, courtyards filled with flowers; boys in an alley hitting a bright blue ball against an old stone wall. My friend will point out to me what had been bombed and what had been spared, saying, *Miracles*. The church bells will ring and ring and ring. The woman will long since have disappeared.

We didn't know where they'd gone, said their neighbors, waking one too-quiet morning to find their neighbors gone — the Jews who had run the village shops; the Gypsies who had made music for generations here. Then not a note, not a scrap of song. Though of course they *knew*. The sky full of smoke. Soon enough, the fields would be char and ash.

And the same thing happens, a young priest in that village will tell me, *the same thing happens and the same thing happens and the same thing happens all over again.* But let this not have happened yet; let it not be happening again.

By dusk, I'll have boarded a train for Warsaw, rushing away from Lodz, alone, clutching my documents in my hand. Thinking: *Who are you who are you who are you? And where are you now, with the violin you made sound like a flock of birds in flight? And the child they'll have torn from your arms —?* Only the sound of iron on iron, wheel on track. And the broken screams. And the bells.

1941: Germany — SS Chief Himmler's deputy Heydrich, chief architect of the Final Solution, announces that the Einsatzkommandos have *received the order to kill all Jews, Gypsies and mental patients.*

Poland — Gypsy camp set up in the Jewish ghetto of Lodz for 5,000 inmates.

1942: Poland — *January:* All Sinti and Roma from the Lodz ghetto are transported and gassed at Chelmo.
— *May:* All Roma from the Warsaw district to be interned in Jewish ghettoes.

1943: Poland — *January:* Roma from Warsaw ghetto transferred to the extermination camp at Treblinka.
— *February:* First transports of Sinti and Roma from Germany are delivered to the new Gypsy Family Section in Auschwitz Birkenau.
— *May:* Nazi doctor Josef Mengele is transferred to Auschwitz and begins his medical experiments on camp inmates, focusing particularly on Roma children, particularly Roma children who are twins.

"He would bring them sweets and toys ... They would call him *Onkel Mengele*. Vera Alexander was a Jewish inmate at Auschwitz who looked after 50 sets of Romani twins: *I remember one set of twins in particular: Guido and Ina, aged about four. One day, Mengele took them away. When they returned ... they had been sewn together, back to back, like Siamese twins. Their wounds were infected and oozing pus. They screamed day and night. Then their parents—I remember the mother's name was Stella—managed to get some morphine and they killed the children in order to end their suffering.*"

— *Michael Berenbaum, <u>The World Must Know:</u>*
<u>The History of the Holocaust as Told in the United</u>
<u>States Holocaust Museum</u>

3 a.m.: dawn already
brightening the sky.
The streets of Krakow
quiet now, although
the birds begin
their singing from
whatever trees there are.
A woman's laughter,
sharp, far off;
the whir of trams,
the ghostly bells.

Today, midday,
I rushed through town —
or was it already
yesterday now?—
and saw that Roma girl
in the passage
I'd given two zlotys to
hours before.
She was licking
an ice cream,
haughty and calm.

"Not real Gypsies,"
my Polish friend said,
"They have big houses
back in Romania."

So, I thought:
*I'll never give anyone
money again.*
Then I saw the boy
who sits all day
in a cardboard box,
the filthy stubs
of his arms.

1943: Poland — *July:* Himmler visits the Gypsy Section in Auschwitz and orders the Roma to be killed.

1944: Poland — *May:* SS guards attempting to liquidate the Gypsy Family Camp are met with unexpected resistance. When ordered to come out, the Roma refuse, arming themselves with iron pipes, shovels, and other tools. The SS withdraw. Some 3,000 Roma capable of forced labor are later transferred to Auschwitz I and other concentration camps.

— *August:* On August 2, the SS moves again against the remaining 2,898 inmates of the Gypsy camp — most of them ill, elderly men, women and children.

1945: Poland — *January:* On January 27 at 3 p.m., soldiers of the 100th Lwów Infantry Division of the 60th Army of the First Ukrainian Front liberate the main camp at Auschwitz and find, among the survivors, one Rom.

They took us in through the gates
They let us out through the chimneys

— Gypsy song

II

No one will speak of this for a long time. In Warsaw and Krakow and Lodz, no one will meet my eyes. The forests of slender birches blur past the windows of the train, seem to offer no shade, no refuge, no possible hiding place. In the quiet, half-empty villages, even the fields seem to turn away.

"Estimates of the death toll of Romanies in World War II range from 220,000 to 1,500,000... There was no Roma representation at the Nuremberg trials. There were no reparations. In 1947, Roma were still living in concentration camps, hiding out. They had no identity papers, and Nazi laws regarding identity were still in effect, so they had no country, nowhere to go."

—*Ian Hancock, from an interview on KPFK, Dec. 2014*

Some say *many*
had escaped.
Some say *no one*
can count them now.

Some, to give a name
to what had happened,
named it *Porajamos,*
the Devouring.

Some for a long time
refused to speak of it
— *Why give them ideas?* —
said nothing at all.

If they were hungry,
there was ash.
If they were thirsty,
there was smoke.

If there was not one bird
to eat,
there was a song,
there was a wheel.
There was a forest,
a river, still.

Some crept out of the depths
of the forests
where they had managed
to survive; some crept,
finally, out of the camps.

Some reported
as had been commanded
to be *accounted for,*
to be settled
in towns and villages
in the fall —

and then, come spring,
whole caravans
disappeared into the night.

1949: USSR & Soviet satellite states — Campaign of Roma settlement begins.

1956: USSR — Supreme Soviet issues *Decree of Nomadic Life Interdiction*.

1958: Bulgaria & Czechoslovakia — Nomadism banned.

1964: Poland — Polish Gypsies forbidden to travel in caravans.

"During 'The Great Halt,' Gypsies were encouraged — or forced, the wooden wheels of their wagons burned on great pyres — to 'settle' in concrete apartment blocks on the outskirts of new Soviet industrial towns like Nowa Huta in southern Poland. Nominally, this settlement was for the purpose of taking a census, of accounting for these unaccountable people...

Opposition to the traveling of Gypsy craftsmen, who had taken their tinsmithing or blacksmithing crafts into the uttermost corners of the country, began gradually to bring about the disappearance of the traditional Gypsy skills in these professions. The disappearance of most of the crafts that they had previously practiced led to a form of social degeneration...

— Ian Hancock, interview on KPFK, Dec. 2014

Vlax Romani Lessons for Rominchals,
Lesson One, *Throat Sounds:*

If you have a Kalderash friend
ask him to say
chorimos, which means stealing
and *chorrimos*, which means poverty.

☏

On ulica Florianska,
a one-legged Gypsy plays violin —
music for pigeons
and for the crowds rushing past,
hurrying to keep warm.
A few coins
in the upturned tambourine.
The violin perched
on the dark boy's shoulder
like a bird he's tamed with string
to sing to us, who are cold
in this wind
that whips down Florianska Street,
tearing its wings from the sky.

1969: Bulgaria — Segregated schools set up for Roma.

1972: Czechoslovakia — Sterilization program for Roma women begins.

The rich confusion of their names:

Atzinganoi: the Greek
from *Athinganoi:* ("heretic")
Zigeuner (German)
(as in: "zig-zag"
as in: "wanders up and down")
Tsigan, Gitane,
Gitano, Gypsy
from *Egyptian*
(as in: "dark-skinned,
foreign, stranger" —
a mistake
appearing first
"the most persistent tag"
in Byzantine poetry)
Gyp comes from *Gypsy*
meaning: "cheat" (cheap
tricks of fortune-tellers, thieves)
Cygane in Polish
which becomes the verb
cyganic: "to deceive"
"One of a dark
Caucasoid people
coming originally from India
to Europe in the fourteenth

or fifteenth century"
Synonym: *Roma*
from the Indic *Rom*
for: "married Gypsy man"
also their language:
Romany
 (the joke: "because we always *roam*")
 (see also *Romani*:
"a blackish-blue
that is redder and less strong
than average midnight")
also: *Nomad; Vagrant*
also: *Traveller*
Asylanten ("asylum-seekers")
Sinti and *Roma*
to the Nazis
(as in: numbered, photographed
as in: rounded up and hanged)
"Perhaps a mixture of all kinds
of rascally people gathered together,
having collectively no certain country"
("home") — *rom*anticized
Romantic, as in: "not conforming
to classical conventions"
as in: "richly imaginative"
Romance: "a picturesque

exaggeration" (meaning: "lie")
also: "a love story"
also: "a love affair
resembling this"

"Among Gypsies, continual self-reinvention has been the primary tool of survival, but the not-knowing has of course had terribly alienating consequences, as did, for example, the forced name-changing in Bulgaria in the late 1980's. Already, many Bulgarian Gypsies cannot remember their own names."

— *Isabel Fonseca, <u>Bury Me Standing</u>*

Bewitched, he says,
this man who *studies Gypsy*,
takes my hand, who's come
with books from Bern by train,
ticks off the languages
he speaks: *Swiss-German,
German, English, French*;
among the Slavic: *Russian,
Serbian, Croatian* — when I ask
if he speaks *Roma*
he says *Romanes*,
corrects me, shakes his head.

(In Basel seven days of snow
have turned the streets into a white map
— muffled, blank —
our breath to smoke.)

He's made the journey here
alone, to meet a stranger *(friend
of friends)* — I watched him climb
the curving staircase
of this steep house from above
(*How young he is,* I thought,
*how handsome, dark —
why was he sent?*)
and said his name
and let him in.

Now we're sitting
in this borrowed kitchen —
my friend, whose home this is,
has said goodnight,
gone to her room —
books and papers strewn
across the table, drinking wine.

He's a scholar, wants to write
about the ways we make ourselves
— *forge an identity* — from words;
about the ways the Romani
are writing their own history
from scratch — *We have to*
make it up, he says,
invent — as I invent myself
(part-Gypsy) laughing,
though my grandmother
left no trace of her path;
though my grandfather was shot
and *I don't have no photograph;*
though there has been
no written history
of Gypsies until now.

It would be nonsense to create
personal mythologies, he says.
His thesis title: *Literary Self-*

*Representation by Roma Writers
in Slavic Languages.*
I think: What tongue
is in his mouth, what tongue
in mine?

(I'd like to write
my name in snow;
I'd like to fly
out of the smoky kitchen, dive
into the blank page
of this Swiss night, disappear.
I'd like to ask him why
he's come, to touch
the language in the air
between us— *only
breath* — his hair.)

And so we talk into the night.
Now: *Is he hungry?* Now:
More wine? Now he confesses
his own grandmother was dark
— *part-Romani?* — and sighs,
turning over in his smooth,
white hands my blood-
red book of poems.

(Well, who can tell?
and who can translate
from a language so few know?)

What I can offer him:
a room in which to sleep
(the trains have stopped) —
the house is many stories
steep and no, not mine —
an empty bed.

At 3 a.m., I say goodnight,
send him down that chilly hallway,
rinse our glasses, slip
into her room to kiss
my sleeping friend *(sweet dreams)*
then climb
the two flights to the loft

— my attic nest beneath the eaves —

and find him waiting there for me:
half in lamplight, half
in shadow, long
frame slouched into a chair beside
the table where I write.

What does he want? — to go on
talking? Or stop talking, take
my wild hair in his hands
and pull me down
into the warmth beneath
the spell of any human
language — *breath* —
which isn't anything
we've named, discussed —
not yet — perhaps
he wants to lick
my name out of my heart.
Perhaps he's young enough
to trust; perhaps he thinks
my strangeness can be drunk
like wine, he's drunk — perhaps
this frozen night I might be loved
if I lay down, unnamed
myself just long enough
to be his *witch*, his *chimera* —

as I have lain down
half my life between
such shimmerings, the stars
burn through the skylights
of the loft in which we talk
and talk and talk —

how long

have Roma erased themselves,
allowed themselves to be erased?

(Ancient history, for most:
the earliest memory of the oldest
one among them, still alive.
Also: a way to hide.
Also: *romanticized to death.)*
How long have I erased myself?

I've kept my name,
my father's name,
his father's name
(who was a ghost)
his mother's name
erased by marriage
and re-marriage,
or by murder, suicide —
her last trace vanishing
like smoke
into the black sky of Detroit;
her only signature
an X — I never thought

to ask my father how
she died or which man
buried her or why
there is no grave.

*We never ask
the things we couldn't bear to know;*
he whispers now —
our voices low
as if to not disturb
the peace, the quiet
night, the clean
white hush
of Switzerland —

beneath the streets of Zurich:
gold — the Nazi loot
of murdered Jews; beneath
the thin veneer of prim
respectability — the truth:
*In 1926, Pro Juventute began a program
of forced removal of Gypsy children
from their families for 'fostering' —*
and Gypsy children sold for cash
by their own parents, governments,
by *pimps* — who wants to write
that kind of history, to tell?

(My grandmother's first marriage
was her sale: thirteen years old
to an old man in the old country —
she must have run from him, escaped.)
Who do we blame? Which parts
of *who we are* do we re-claim, erase?

For years, I've rushed alone
down wind-swept streets,
been swept along — hurried
through the stations of strange cities
— followed, lost —
and flown into the arms
of men who've held me, whispered:
witch, bewitched, enchanted —
let me go.

(There is a man in Paris now
who calls me *ma petite Gitane*;
a man who says:
too powerful for me,
draws back his hands;
a man, American,
who writes: *No country
can hold you, so how
could any man?*

In every city I have ever loved
a man who makes me
out of air, his breath
erasing me again.)

And this man has a wife
in Bern (*not 'wife,'* he says)
(then: *sweetheart*); child —
and he'll return to them,
return to what he knows
is *real*, is *home*.

So when he stands, at last
to go, I stand up, too:
it's nearly dawn.
We say each other's names
and laugh. We say:
we'll meet again; we'll write.

Perhaps he'll dream
of how I'd taste, dissolve
like language on his tongue.
I'll dream we dive
into the snow, so deep
we swim through drifts of blue;
a lit fuse woven
in my hair, the wild
sparks inextinguishable.

Think of him: rushing
through the bruised and silver light
to catch his train;
his breath before him, cold
and untranslatable, my red book
in the pocket of his coat.

If I could touch
a single word
I'd set it flaming in his hand.

1986: Spain — Romani houses set on fire in Martos.

1989: Germany — Government initiates the deportation of several thousand Roma from the country.

1992: Ukraine — Mob attacks Romani houses in Tatarbunary.

1992: Germany — Government 'sells' Romani asylum seekers back to Romania for $21 million, and begins shipping them in handcuffs on November 1.

1993: Former Yugoslavia — As war in the Balkans gathers pace, many Roma flee to avoid conscription. Others targeted by military on various sides.

Each day Dana listens
for the news of war
from home —ex-
Yugoslavia — pronounces it
a cross drawn through a name.
She's black-eyed,
Bosnian, a Serb —
though she's lived for twenty years
among the angels of Berlin,
among the ruins made into monuments
and knows her way around:
knows the trains
that run beneath the streets,
the ghost wall
where the wall once stood
—*partition*—
and the restaurants
where we'll be served *like queens*
— Croatian, Serb, Slovenian —
These are my friends,
she says, my friend
who toasts the living
and the dead, sighs,
my rivers and my mountains,
mourns, *my country* —
can't go back

because it no longer exists,
never existed *(none of us*
knows who our real grandfathers were.)
So she laughs
her dark laugh, lights
her thousand-thousandth cigarette,
calls me her *Gypsy cousin*, dreams
a black line runs right down the center
of her body like a map;
wakes to tell me:
I have two selves, Ceily,
so which one I am?

> "Oh Europe is so many borders
> on every border, murderers"
> — *Attila Josef, Hungarian Poet*

All night crossing the Tatra,
Krakow to Budapest, the train
only three cars long — where is my friend?
Ken, who calls me *Regina Cecylia,*
Queen of the Gypsies, Carpathia.
We've travelled together from Berlin
but now the dining car between our cars
is locked — I can't get through.
In these couchettes, only one other woman,
the small boy who clings to her, hiding his face,
and the porter who's taken my ticket,
refuses in Polish to give it back.

Lie down then, let this pass:
the window a square of black glass
in which bare trees, fields appear;
forests where I could be left,
this car uncoupled — who would know?
(500,000 Gypsies burned in the crematoria)
At each border *(which country now?)*
a clapboard shack with its plume of smoke
and the guards in their high boots,

their stink of cigar, who throw back
the door of my compartment, flick
on the lights, demand documents.

What if I had no passport, no papers
to prove I'm American?
What if I'd been born
in the village my grandmother fled?
What if I had no country —
would I be no one, then, to them?
Would they drag me into the woods;
would the quiet woman hold her child
a little closer, cover his ears?

Sleeping and waking and sleeping again;
disappearing into the dream, waking into the dream
of Budapest: it's snowing so softly
the golden domes that crown the city seem to float.
At dawn, the grim porter reappears
with black coffee, sugar, two hard rolls,
my ticket, crumpled, on the tray.

I jump off the train with my suitcase
into the station's soot and din,
into the arms of ragged men —
Gypsies everywhere, suddenly, flocks of them,
chanting like sorcerers, surrounding me,
calling out, *Taxi! Taxi! Room!*

I've read that, in caverns under these stations
— Sofia, Bucharest, Budapest —
Gypsy orphans live on glue, pimped
for candy, for cigarettes.
But no children greet me here —
only these dark men I turn from, refuse,
and my tall friend, rushing toward me
down the crowded platform now:
silently, given back, at last,
my name in his throat like a jewel.

☙

What if you lived in a box, in a tree, in a car by the side of the road? What if your shoes were full of rain and mud and you stank like the dog you loved? What if you slept every night in a different ditch, were always cold? What if you had no coat but the coat you'd stolen, rag and wind? What if you kept moving to keep warm and kept warm by burning what you had? What if you bathed in poisoned rivers, drank from them, ate their fish? What if you crossed at dusk into a country clamping down? What if they called you *Gypsy*, *nomad*, meant: *not wanted here*? What if they tried to wipe you like a dark stain from the map? What if you lived in a tree, a box, a car? What if you lived?

1994: **Britain** — Criminal Justice Act: Nomadism criminalized.

1995: **Austria** — Four Roma killed by a bomb in Oberwat, Burgenland.
Hungary — Roma attacked in Kalocza.
Poland — Romani couple murdered in Pablanice. Grota Bridge settlement of Romanian Gypsies in Warsaw is raided and its residents deported across the border to Ukraine.
Slovakia — Mario Goral, a Rom, burnt to death by skinheads in Ziar nad Hronom.
Bulgaria — One Rom dies following an arson attack on a block of flats in Sofia. Angel Angelov, a Rom, shot by police in Nova Zagora.

Los Angeles again:
November and the sky
keeps shifting,
radiant and blank.
I'm driving south
along the curving freeway, straight
into the heart
of this, *Our Lady, Queen
of Angels* —
but the heart
keeps shifting, too:
the gleaming towers
seem to rise and fall
and shimmer, seem to float
within the haze
of milky sunlight
—city drifting in its veils—
how have I lived
half of my life
half-exiled here
(*just passing through*)
and never stopped to ask:
what keeps me coming back?
or called it *home*?

The skyline tilts,
swerves into view
then disappears
between the hills
behind the walls
scrawled dark with threats —
wild hieroglyphics
of the gangs
who mark the borders
of their territories — *this
is mine* — and this
is how the world
will not divide
(*the lines on maps
are only lines*)
will not stay blank
(they're painted out;
the wild scrawls
reappear at dawn.)

And down the canyons
burning gold
of winter sunlight,
waves of sound
that travel all around the world
and through our bodies,

ghost-like, whole
until they shatter
into voices
we can hear —
the radio:
> *in the former Yugoslavia*
> *in Belgrade*
> *in the streets*
> *neo-Nazi skinhead groups*
> *(mostly kids*
> *with nothing else to do)*
> *beat Gypsies*
> *murder them*

This comes from
Washington, this comes
from further east —
Belgrade itself.
The voices weary
with despair discuss
who dies?
The calm report:
> *two years since the Dayton*
> *Peace Accord*
> *the rise of street gang*
> *violence against Gypsies living*

in Serbia, a rise
of neo-Nazi skinhead groups
that go around in the streets
of Belgrade at night
attacking Gypsies
attacking the street cleaners
who work at night
most of whom are Gypsies
stripping them of their clothes
making them walk home naked
holding them down
lighting their hair on fire

a pregnant woman
with three children
beaten to death

this boy who had just
gone down to the corner
store to buy some juice
these skinheads ripped
a drain pipe off the wall
beat him to death

this boy who was fourteen

*and they don't have
the light touch
in Belgrade*

This news is
news? Who else
is listening? The sky
like broken glass
through which *light
touches* everything;
the traffic gleaming,
rushing south
becomes a stream
in which the sound
of any human voice
would drown;
and then a river
flowing, bright
into the sea of mirrors,
clouds, in which
the angels of a city
I have never loved
spread out —

in which police
have blocked
the northbound lanes,

lights flashing,
traffic clogged —
a body fallen
from the overpass
or someone chose
to leap
into the rush
of shine and speed,
the crushing river,
made it stop —

the cops in prayer
(what seems like prayer)
around the stretcher,
each head bowed
— a homeless man?
a desperate kid?
*(Please let him not
be dead,* I think)
a shape beneath the sheet
— no movement, breath —
as we slide past
so slowly now:
what kind of heartsick
ritual is this?

And now a face
behind each wheel,
each one a witness
— human, shocked —
What we don't see
must not exist:
the other city —
subterranean — within
the shadowed grid
where those who live
in cardboard boxes,
freeway underpasses, piss
in doorways, warm themselves
at grates, lie down
along the fences
of this world, build fires,
wait —

or fling themselves,
angelic, from the sky
in front of us.

Our silence shattered
into deeper silence; words
come back to me:

a Jew, a doctor
who survived
the camp at Auschwitz,
who described
the final days before
the Nazis fell in 1945:
how the kripo came every day
ordering Gypsies to hang their kin
(for whom kin
was the only country
they had ever
lived within.)

The sirens keen,
the traffic crawls
into the underpasses, snarled
along the bridges flung
in weightless arcs between
the gleaming towers
—a grim processional—
as if we slow to mourn
what dies in us.

The words I've read
and read again until
I'm numb with facts
are facts:

since 1989, all over
Romania, Transylvania,
Gypsy settlements burned down;
good Christians ringing
churchbells: *Now those Roma
won't act so proud*;
Gypsy orphans
living in train stations,
in tunnels underground;
Kalderash women on streetcorners
selling contraceptives, knives —
despised for their poverty,
their indifference
to *the sanctity of property,*
their own unwritten history,
the purity of nations, states —

they trespass into cities
darkly, fly away again:

*"not so much nomadic by nature
as that they were never
allowed to stay"*

How have I lived
this many years,
come this far west,

swept through, returned
and never known
what my own freedom meant,
or exile,
homelessness?
How do I live
inside this history,
wheel slipping
through my hands? —

> *they were slaves in Wallachia*
> *until the 1800's*
> *hunted down:*
> *a Gypsy woman*
> *with an infant at her breast;*
> *a lovely teenage girl*
> *sold to an old man*
> *for a single piece*
> *of silver* — my own
> grandmother was given up
> like this.

Our treaties make no claims
for those who claim
no nation, *home*;
who live in washrooms

in the train stations
of Warsaw and Berlin,
trying to get from any
place to any place—
The West —

and still it's never
far enough
to fly, I think
of how I've flown
across the world
and never found
a single line
that I could trace
(*the lines on maps
are only lines*)
a name that answered
to my name,
a place that held me
hard between its borders,
whispered to me:
stay.

And now the city
drifts behind me
in the mirror — *chimera* —
as if transparent, after all

(oh pure idea: nation, state)
as if by crossing
and re-crossing I could
wear the borders down
or smudge my thumb
across the map
with spit and ash
until there's nothing left
(the pavement stained
with blood) —

as if I've plunged
into the heart
of this, *Our Lady, Queen
of Angels,* risen up
to fly again —*Tsiganka,
Gypsy* that I am,
wheeling and turning
west and west
until west turns
to east again,
until I've circled back
to *home*, to where
the world, at last,
begins.

1997: **Romania** — Mob attacks Romani houses in Tananu village.
Ukraine — Roma beaten by police in four separate incidents in Uzhorod.
Bulgaria — Police attack the Romani quarter in Pazardjik.
France — Jose Menager and Manolito Meuche, two Roma, shot dead by police in Nantes.
Greece — Eviction of 100 Romani families from Ano Liosia. Partial resettlement in guarded camp.
Poland — Roma attacked in Wiebodzice.
Czech Republic — Several hundred Roma fly to Canada to seek asylum.
Norway — Romani people are awarded the Rafto Human Rights Prize.

My great-uncle, seventy-three years old,
sits at the kitchen table and sobs.
He was a boy when his father sent him
into the streets of Pittsburgh to beg.
*We were so poor. There was nothing
to eat.* Still, the shame burns in him, still,
sixty years after the fact he wants not
to remember — *Oh honey, honey*, he says,
no one wants to remember that stuff —
who turned away from him, who
turned away, who was only a boy
on the streets of America, begging
for mercy, now, begging me *please* —
wanting me not to have asked
what I've asked, what I've always asked:
who we are, how we've come to be here
in my cousin's kitchen, the table between us
laden with more than we can eat.

> *"I go where I love*
> *and where I am loved*
> *into the snow*
>
> *I go where I love*
> *and where I am loved*
> *with no thought*
> *of duty or pity"*
>   — H.D.

Twilight: moving east
en route to Krosno, moving south
toward that corner of the map
where Poland, Ukraine, Slovakia touch —
the upper curve of the crescent moon
of the northernmost Carpathians.

(The Lemki, Wallachians — nomads —
followed the curve of this crescent, traveled
the peaks from Romania, never descending
into the valleys — *notorious tribes.*)

Alone on a train on my way to friends
who've written: *maybe we can find*
your grandmother's village; maybe it's here.

(Shift the old borders, shift a few letters
of the name of the town one great-uncle remembered—
But why would you want to go there?)

Pressing my face against the window, facing
backwards (*to see where we've been*);
the stations we pass becoming less
and less like stations as we pass:
gray concrete walls giving way to shacks
beside the tracks, then weed-choked lots
then just a rusted sign, a bench —
(*Will I know where to step off the train
in the dark? How will I know where I am?*)

Eight hours from Warsaw the vestibule reeks
of cold wind, piss; the iron wheels screech.
Young soldiers, drunk, lurch arm-in-arm
down the narrow passageways, stagger
on and off the train, their voices raised
in some dark song — *but what are they singing?
Where are we now?*

No common language: the other passengers
(fewer and fewer the further we go) murmur
in Polish or not at all; silently smoke
in the dim yellow light of their compartments
— no way to ask: *Is this the place?*

Is this? Is this? (Three different stations
called *Krosno* — *which?*)
or quiet the fear that I'm disappearing
into this landscape, might not reappear.

In every direction now: colorless fields
cut down to stubble, sharp with frost
and here and there a patch of blackened snow,
a smudge of oily smoke — a fire blazing,
sudden gold against the sky's deep empty blue
(*What are they burning? Where do they live?*)
— no town or village, barn or shelter,
human dwelling; *place to rest.*

And then I see her, with her dark brood,
moving swiftly down the tracks:
a woman walking, bundle slung
across one shoulder (bright rags, sticks)
and (count them) children — five or six —
a flock of blackbirds, following.

I look up just in time to catch her eye;
she catches mine — we catch each other
vanishing: the train all iron and spark and speed;
her long skirt dragging in the mud. I press
my palm against the cool glass,
thinking: *how, where will we sleep?*

"Historically, they have been accused of child stealing. This has to be nonsense, if for no other reason than that they always have plenty of kids of their own and that being caught at this would almost certainly have invited a pogrom and perhaps local extermination. The grim historical truth seems to have been that the Gypsies were made scapegoats for the practice of infanticide by desperate peasant women for whom child murder was the only available form of birth control."

— *"Gypsies," By Stephen Browne; Warsaw Insider, May 2000*

We didn't have anything, my mother says.
We were poor; everyone was poor back then.
No one had car seats for babies; I just held you in my arms.
So I was new-born, it was Thanksgiving day,
and probably swaddled in pink in the crook
of my mother's girlish arm.
And of course there would be no cradle
in my father's teta's house.
We just opened a drawer, you were so small
and they lay me down among linens, clothes —
a nest I'd remember if memory served
to keep us just this safe, this warm.
I talk to my mother over the phone
across a distance of thousands of miles.
I lean back in a shaft of sunlight, listen:
this is her voice, this is home.

1998: U.S.A. — Last existing U.S. law discriminating against Roma is rescinded in New Jersey.

The oldest woman in Wislok Wielki
is only a voice
from a farther room
saying, *Nye* and *Nye*
from behind the wall
of the bright, neat kitchen where we sit —
my friend and the priest and I
having come this far,
having come so near.
But she's never heard of us,
she is saying, *Vol-ock?*
Nye and *Nye* and *Nye*.
And then I write
my grandmother's maiden name
on a scrap of paper, push
the scrap of paper across
the table toward my friend,
who passes it to the priest,
who pronounces it:
Bakasae, Maria.

In the doorway a tiny figure appears
(*so gorgeous*, my friend will say later,
I could have fallen to my knees):
her skin the bronze
of autumn leaves; her hair

a shock of silver-white beneath
a scarf of emerald green.
And she's nodding her head,
saying, *Tak*, saying, *Yes*
and the young priest's eyes go wide
and my friend says, *She says
she remembers that family* —
and then she's disappeared again —

light in strange arcs
falling onto my hands
and the whole village breathless,
waiting, still.

I'm standing in light rain in early May in back of the church of St. Nicholas, in the village of Olchowiec, in the lower Carpathians. A small crowd has gathered, here, between the wooden church and the old stone bridge and the graveyard that spreads up the hillside into the trees. A candle flickering on each grave; so that, now, in the soft gray dusk, the hillside seems covered in faint gold stars.

Or have I only imagined this?

A place where the grass is lush and damp. Where a few dozen men and women, a few children, stand or crouch or kneel on the ground. They've formed a quiet half-circle around me, listening while I read aloud. While I say the poem that says this place might not exist in this very place: *only a line on the map, an invisible line, erased.* Those around me smiling, now, or tilting their heads to one side, probably not understanding a word.

Or have we dreamed one another here?

Below, in a meadow beyond a chain-link fence, a bonfire is being lit. Smoke rising into the air; a few notes; the musicians already tuning up. And the one Gypsy family left in this village —the one family not sent away to the

camps or, sent away, who survived and came back —
beginning, already, to dance. If you listen, you'll hear the
violins. If the dead are listening, even my father, even his
mother and all the others, beloved and dreamt of, are
dreaming this: the words in my mouth as sweet as rain;
my head tipped back to taste them, sing.

☙

Before I was born, she died —
traced a question mark over her heart
instead of crossing herself, and collapsed.
Who took the long black car,
the cocky hats, the documents?
Years rolled past and years
were lost to the weather before I came.
Here is your girl, said the world
but my grandmother wasn't listening.
She was too far dead, by then,
she was too far over the edge of her life.
This was a trick she had down to an art:
vanishing, standing there like that.
Flick of her knife and the candle goes out —
darkness; I've burned my hand on the wax.
She waited as long as she could, she says,
but my father was stubborn, my mother was young.
And the world, which had given her sons
then killed them one by one, left two,
saying, *These boys will make good meat*
and put them in cages for a while.
That's when she licked the last thread
on the last of her beautiful burial shrouds.
Go ahead, she hissed to the shadows
falling over her like clocks.

So I was born on a white afternoon
in the middle of winter,
given the blank page of her death
on which to write my history.

☙

We were going by train we were going by plane we were going by ship by bicycle. We were going on foot we were going in rain we were going by bridge by car alone. We were always the same strange woman with our one black suitcase packed. We were moving in some kind of subtle direction on a smudged map, dark with crows. But without compass schedule plans — we were losing everything we passed. We were throwing happiness with both hands to the wind like ragged clothes. We were searching for the underground of everywhere at once. We looked into the mirror of the road for signs of god. We were often photographed. We were never captured. Not for long. We were going where the suffering was best to suffer more. And where the joy was blinding, too. We were wearing veils beneath our veils. We were lapping up the world and rushing through it as it slept. We were multiple as stars as grass the ghostly barren trees. We were a single moving shape: shadow and flesh, the shape between. I thought I saw you once over my shoulder, felt you breathe. I ran and ran. Someone was panting down the tracks. Our arms were wings.

*Even the sparrow finds a home
and the swallow a nest for herself ...*

Psalm 84:3

III Coda

I COME TO YOU
(me jawjom ki tume) 1953

I haven't come to you to get something to eat.
I come to you to believe me.
I haven't come to you to get money from you.
I come so that you give it all away.
I come to you from ragged tents,
torn by wind, taken by water.
I beg you all, I beg the old,
I beg little children, and beautiful girls,
build houses as silver as tents,
that you can see in the forest whitened by frost!
I haven't come to you to get money from you.
I come so that you could receive everybody,
so that you would not make a dark night
out of a sunny day.

Bronislawa Wajs, the Roma poet known as Papusza

2005: Alfreda Moska, a Polish Roma who survived the massacre of her family by the Nazis in 1941 and went on to save at least 50 Roma and Jewish children, is awarded the Commander's Cross with Star of the Order of Polonia Restituta for *heroism and exceptional courage.*

There are so many stories, she says, her hands aflutter, dispirited. Her Jewish grandfather killed by the Nazis; her husband's Nazi grandfather killing himself at the end of the war. All the children who were orphaned, abandoned, given up, given to someone else. Who survived and who didn't survive. The Jewish artist who drew portraits of the Roma in the camps. The 92-year-old Rom we met this evening, who escaped from camps nine different times and *lived to tell.* But who's listening now?

And how will we tell all these stories, we ask, and still tell the stories of ourselves? How will we connect the past to the future, without getting lost? With the present all around us, now, and indecipherable.

Today, I stepped off a train in Krakow into the swirl of a shopping mall. Confused by all the bright colors, the cacophony, the crowds. I wanted the old city rising up out of the blue-grey mist again, when nothing much was for sale, when everyone was so poor that we mattered to one another more. But I found my way, somehow, into the leafy summer dusk. *Just let us not be dead again*, I thought. Then I hurried to meet my friend.

(for Gabi Von Seitmann, Krakow, July 2017)

2005: Decade of Roma Inclusion begins, an initiative of 12 European countries to "close the gaps between Roma and the rest of society."

2008: Amnesty International reports that one in five of all Roma in Europe have been subjected to racially motivated crime in the previous year.

2010: Some 10,000 Roma expelled from France.

2012: On Easter Sunday, in Rome, the Vatican removes 150 Roma who had taken shelter in the church, St. Paul's Beyond the Walls, after their camps were broken down by the Italian government. There had been a fire in which four children burned to death.

2014: In France, a 17-year-old Roma boy is beaten unconscious by a gang of 20 men wielding wooden and metal sticks, his limp body dumped in a shopping cart.

September 23 — Raymond Gurême, 89-year-old survivor of the persecution of Roma in France during World War II, and veteran of the French Resistance, assaulted in his home in Arpajon by a French policeman.

2015: Decade of Roma Inclusion ends.

"I was hiding in a tree the whole night while the police were looking for me."
—Raymond Gurême, in an interview with the Brussells Times, April 8, 2015

He doesn't say they'd tried to kill him, but they had. A face like smoke. A wraith. A man who was a boy who disappeared, escaped again. Now he sits beneath a tree outside the gates of the concentration camp and lights a cigarette.

He was an acrobat, he says to me in French. And still so slight, so lithe — *You see?* He locks his hands behind his back and shows me how he bent in two, stepped through those shackles, slipped away. *Gave them the slip* nine different times, was only caught eight times, brought back. He's ninety-two years old and smokes a cigarette beneath a tree in Auschwitz, says, *You see?*

Against the monsters of the world, this little man, his black hat cocked. Once, the plump guards laughed, *made merry*, while the likes of this man starved. Now, we pass some sandwiches around. What isn't over has begun again. We're hungry, but there's more. The grass grows lush with human ash. There are no birds — no, there's one bird.

(Auschwitz-Birkenau, July 31, 2017)

Un oiseau, I cry out, when a bird flies past —
the only bird we've seen all day. Then the word
for *bird* in several other languages flies up —
a flock of words, like birds, for *bird*. As if
by naming it, we make that bird a bird, a sky for it.

We're sitting in a circle in the lush grass in the shade,
near where the crematorium stood, here, where the fields
had turned to mud because *they'd eaten all the grass* —
those who were starved before they were gassed,
then burned; here, where the smoke of their bodies rose.

All day, the sun has been hot, a naked sun, a sun of bone.
We've walked in silence through the *Zigeunerlager*,
the Gypsy Family Camp, past barracks and barbed wire,
my young friends wearing t-shirts printed: *to look and not
forget*. That *their kind* were murdered in this place.

One of the young men in the circle begins to weep.
How did this happen, he wants to know —asking
in which of our languages? Someone translates
his words into French, then someone translates
the words into English. Then someone turns to me.

But we're here, I say, *You're here. I look at you.*
I look at them. Their beautiful faces turning toward me

in the slowly goldening light. Their beautiful faces turning toward one another in that light. And they see themselves. I see. And in that gaze, a kind of prayer.

"They died on the roads of their wandering, they died in their sheltered forests, but above all, they died here — on the land where you stand today.

At this place, people of different nationalities, religions, orientations died. The presence of representatives of various countries in today's ceremony, for which I am deeply grateful, highlights the universal aspect of Auschwitz — the place where the ultimate attempt was made to deny the unity of the human family."

— *Roman Kwiatkowski, Chairman of the Roma People Association in Poland, Auschwitz-Birkenau, August 2, 2017*

You must find your people, the driver said,
leaving me off in a place that seemed unfamiliar,
where I didn't see anyone at all — an empty street,
an empty lawn, a gray building grim as a bunker,
I thought — *But where was everyone?*

And then a crowd came spilling out
into the morning light, my friends,
and I knew where I was again.

A long, quiet bus ride from Krakow to Auschwitz.
Then a long, quiet walk into the camp.
The young man in front of me wore a Roma flag
draped over his shoulders like a cape:
red wheel on a field of blue and green.

They let us in through the gates,
They let us out through the chimneys.
Roses heaped where there were no graves.

A man spoke of being a child here,
hungry, limp, on his mother's knees.
A woman remembered her godmother,
her godmother's husband, their five little girls,
who all *went up in smoke*.

In the hell of Auschwitz where real devils
lived in human skin.
We walked out under a scorching sun.

In the evening, in the garden of the *Tsiganaria*,
I danced with a man who tried to tell me,
in halting English, his father's life:
a Rom who'd served in the German army,
denounced by his landlord — *Who be you?* —

he was sent to Auschwitz, nearly starved;
came home alive, but sick and thin —
so thin, he died in months.

His plump son twirled me and kissed my hand.
God please you, he said to me, and smiled.
The moon rose-gold above the trees.
We're here, just look at us.
God, please.

Author's Note (Second Edition)

I was born in Pittsburgh, Pennsylvania, and grew up there and in rural Kentucky, the second of seven children of a homemaker and an airplane mechanic. My mother came from a large, close-knit family that identified as Polish-American. My father's people — always very secretive and mysterious — came from a place I only ever heard identified as "the Carpathians." They seemed afraid that something dangerous and even damning might be revealed if they were more specific about our origins. My paternal great-aunts and great-uncles sometimes whispered about our "Gypsy blood," but couldn't or wouldn't say more. My mother joked about it, but darkly, referring to my father's relatives as *the outlaws*; my father called me *Tsiganka, little Gypsy*, which was what his mother had been called.

My father's mother, who had come to the U.S. around 1910, was a mystery within a mystery. She seemed to have vanished without a trace before I was born. Whatever had happened to her wasn't discussed openly when I was growing up, but I was always told that I was "just like her," especially in regard to my restlessness, my penchant for travel and, later, my interest in the Tarot deck. My grandmother had "read the cards;" she had been the midwife and barber and mortician in her village in the old country — some kind of shamaness, it seemed. And in the new country, at some point, she had taken to disappearing in a long black car, not telling anyone where she went. My father's father — the first (or second) of my grandmother's three (or four) husbands — had been shot by a policeman on a Pittsburgh street before my father was born. There was subsequently never any contact with that side of the family, and so that part of our lineage is yet another mystery. Although the surname my grandfather left to us hints at roots in the part of Romania once called Wallachia, where the Gypsies known as *Vlach-Roma* were slaves until the mid-1800's.

But coming of age in the U.S. in the 1960's and 1970's, whatever images I had of Gypsies were positive: Gypsies made music, they danced, they traveled; they represented freedom and creativity and high-spiritedness; they were exotic and "other." Those romantic stereotypes were highly attractive to a rebellious daughter of rebel parents, a dark child from a large, unruly family that didn't seem to "fit in" in America. I couldn't understand why the possibility of having "Gypsy blood" should be a source of secrecy or shame. Since there was also a sense of secrecy around my grandmother, I wondered if having been a Gypsy might explain how or why she'd vanished. At some point, I heard a rumor that she'd either committed suicide or been murdered — or I dreamed that I'd heard that rumor. My grandmother, like the Gypsies, seemed to me for a long time more mythological than real, and compellingly mysterious. Although I couldn't have explained why, I began to think that both mysteries might be solved — the mystery of our "Gypsy blood," and of my grandmother's disappearance — if I could only find the place she had come from, in the Carpathians, which I also thought might not really exist.

I had begun to travel, usually solo, when I was a teenager. In my twenties, I had caught glimpses of Gypsies in Spain and Italy and France that had pierced the bubble of my romantic notions. Then, in the early 1990's, I began to travel further east, into the central European countries that had been part of the Soviet Bloc. I saw Gypsy families living in the washrooms of train stations, Gypsy children begging; I heard the wounding slurs that were used against them and felt wounded, too. And eventually, as I'd half-believed and hoped they would, my travels led me to the Carpathian village in the borderlands of southeastern Poland where my grandmother had been born, Wislok Wielki. I learned that, during her youth, Roma and other people of nomadic origin — Lemkos and Vlachs — as well as Jews, had lived together there. That was the village my grandmother had left when she'd emigrated to America. Later, during WWII, when the village was occupied by German troops, those who were identified as Jews and Roma "disappeared;" the remaining inhabitants were forcibly evacuated by Polish Communist troops during Operation Wisla in 1947 — a tragically effective case of ethnic cleansing, although the village still exists as a shadow of its former self.

That's almost all I know about that rumor of "Gypsy blood" and my ancestral link to the Roma. The family in which I grew up was clannish and unconventional, a family with habits I've since heard described as "typically Roma." I didn't grow up in a Roma community, however, so I'm not at all sure I can make any claim to Roma identity. But Roma identity is, itself, mysterious and difficult to pin down; and, through my travels and my research about my family's history, I've come to distrust group identities that rely on geographical borders or claims to ethnic purity. Because Roma identity doesn't rely on the Fascist idea of "blood and soil," it's the only collective identity I care to embrace. For me, it's a spiritual embrace, a stance toward, and in, the world. A Roma friend once said to me, "Being a Gypsy isn't a matter of blood; it's a state of soul."

I wrote *Tsigan: The Gypsy Poem* from that spiritual

impulse, and from a desire to understand the Gypsies' history, and my own — a desire that became an obsession — and as a chronicle of the travels that led me back to that Carpathian village.

In 1997, I had published my first book of poems. A mentor who noticed me carrying around Isabelle Fonseca's book, *Bury Me Standing: The Gypsies and Their Journey*, suggested that I explore my obsession with the Gypsies in a long poem in linked sections. Fonseca's book had provided the first glimmer of the travails and persecution of Gypsies throughout Europe and throughout history. At the time, there was little other material available to me in English; the internet was still in its adolescence, and my research skills left much to be desired. But friends in Europe who were aware of my project provided what information they could, and they put me in touch with their friends. A friend of a friend in England gave me a copy of *The Roads of the Roma*; the poetry in that collection, and the timeline assembled by editors Siobhan Dowd, Rajko Djuric and Ian Hancock, inspired and informed me. I began to see a bigger picture that reflected, however obscurely, my family's shadowy history and my own journey.

Yet, as I wrote the poems that I would weave together into *Tsigan*, my sense was that this was a very personal project, one that, if ever published, would be of little interest to anyone beyond my immediate family. I had no intention or hope of speaking for the Roma people, only of creating a kind of document for my brothers and sisters, a story in which we might belong, one that might help to explain us to ourselves. Although I was wary, too, of the response of my elders, since those intimations of "Gypsy blood," in my understanding, were not to be spoken of outside the family circle.

By the time *Tsigan* was published in early 2002, my father had passed away, as had most of his aunts and uncles. My mother, however, much to my surprise, loved the book. "I only worry," she told me, "about you traveling the way you do, now that you're a *public* Gypsy." I didn't ask her to explain. She died a few years later, so I'll never know what she meant by that statement or what she knew about that part of our history. More recently, when I asked an elderly relative of my father's if the rumors might be true, she shrugged and said, "Of course there's Gypsy blood."

It's also become increasingly clear to me, as I've continued my research, that my grandmother — called *Marushka* and *Tsiganka* —was in fact murdered, in 1949, in Detroit, at the height of the Red Scare. I'm fairly certain that her murder had something to do with her political activities, and that her political activities had their source in that ancestral village in the Carpathians, with its complicated history and politics and shifting identities. So, while I'd thought that finding Wislok Wielki, in 1999, was the end of a long search, it was really only another beginning.

That *Tsigan* has taken on a life of its own, in the fifteen years since it was published, has been astonishing and gratifying to me. In 2013, while I was on the creative writing faculty at the University of Southern California, the university's Visions and Voices Initiative sponsored a multi-media presentation of the text in collaboration with the Shoah Foundation Archives. The presentation included excerpts from filmed testimonies of Roma survivors of WWII concentration camps. For most of the several hundred members of the audience, this was their first encounter with the history of the Roma in the Holocaust. After the presentation, audience members engaged in a discussion with special guests Ian Hancock, co-editor of *Roads of the Roma*, linguist, scholar and activist, and Stephen Smith, executive director of the Shoah Foundation. In 2014, a French translation of *Tsigan* was published by Scribe l'Harmattan; bilingual (French and English) presentations have been staged by la Compagnie Erinna in Paris, Montpellier and Faverges, France. In early 2015, the Museum of the History of Polish Jews in Warsaw sponsored a bilingual multi-media presentation of *Tsigan* as part of its commemoration of International Holocaust Remembrance Day.

Partly as a result of the work I undertook to adapt the text for these presentations, and partly as a result of continuing research, I came to see a gap in the narrative of *Tsigan* that I felt I could bridge, incorporating material that hadn't been available to me in the late 1990's. Furthermore, while I've wanted to remain true to the original impulse and trajectory of the poem, the fact is that history hasn't stood still, nor have I. Originally, *Tsigan* ended on what might be called a "high note" — the rescinding of the last anti-Gypsy law in the U.S. in 1998, and my encounter, the following year, at a festival near the village of my grandmother's birth, with a family of Carpathian Roma who'd survived the Nazi death camps and returned to the area. Yet, across Europe, the Roma people have continued to be misjudged and, especially in the current atmosphere of nationalism and xenophobia, persecuted and marginalized. Meanwhile, the poem itself has given me entree into communities of Roma artists, activists and scholars who have done much to enrich my awareness. I'm grateful beyond words for the way I've been welcomed, even embraced, by Roma communities in Europe.

I'm also painfully aware of the controversy

around the use of the terms "Tsigan" and "Gypsy," as well as other names for the Roma people. (See "The rich confusion of their names.") How to identify a people so diverse and yet so distinct, whose culture, language, history and identity seem to have always been so fluid, so difficult to categorize? I have argued with a (non-Roma) French translator, who insisted that the *Gitanes* of Spain bear no relation to the *Roma* of the rest of Europe. I've been told by a Roma poet in Romania that the words *Tsigan* and *Gypsy* are "terrible" words, with terrible associations, that only the term *Roma* is acceptable. A Roma poet from the U.K. urged me: "Go ahead, be brave, and use the word *Gypsy*" — the term by which he identifies himself. The leader of the Cirque Tzigane in Paris told me he was glad that I'd used the word *Tsigan* for the title of my poem. "That's who we are," he said, "this *Roma* is the invention of academics." And then there are terms like *Nomad* and *Traveler*, which seem to indicate a lifestyle choice more than an ethnic or cultural identity.

    Two considerations, in the end, have taken precedence for me, in regard to this naming: first, the fact that the nickname my father gave to me as a child, *Tsiganka*, was a term of endearment and affection, intended to acknowledge and honor my connection to my lost grandmother; secondly, that the term *Gypsy* is the term best understood in the U.S., where persecution of the Roma people has been minimal compared to the persecution Roma have experienced in Europe. In the U.S., the word *Gypsy* has (albeit highly romanticized) positive associations, in the minds of most people, with creativity, music and freedom; while the word *Roma* is little known and not well understood. Especially in the U.S., its use sows further confusion, as many Americans associate the term *Roma* with Romania, or with Rome,

Italy. So, I choose the term *Gypsy* because it seems to me more comprehensible to my audience, more accessible and more inclusive, and *Tsigan* for its personal relevance in my own life. I hope that those who are offended by these terms will understand and forgive me.

It's also my hope that, by using the terms *Gypsy* and *Tsigan*, alternating their use with the use of the terms *Roma* and *Romani*, as well as *Sinti, Gitane, Nomad, Traveler*, I might familiarize my readers with how fluid and complicated and sometimes wounding this naming has been. As I understand it, the word *Gypsy* evolved, etymologically, from the belief that the early Roma in Europe had come by way of Egypt – inaccurate, possibly, but not necessarily derisive. Likewise, if the word *Tsigan* evolved from a Germanic term indicating people whose travel traced a *zigzagging* course, it seems to me more descriptive than derisive. And if a word can become a slur by dint of the way it's used, might it be possible to rescue a word by using it with respect and even love?

I realize the dangers of confusing a human being with a metaphor, but I also believe that metaphors have real power. If, as the poet W.S. Merwin suggested to me, the image of the Gypsy, in *Tsigan: The Gypsy Poem*, becomes a metaphor for the poem, itself, and for creative fire, for the spirit, it might also be a metaphor for the part of human nature that resists institutionalization and classification. That part of our nature —which doesn't fit neatly between any borders — seems to inspire fear and hatred in those who seek a sense of security through order, conformity and control. What I'd like to ask, through my poem, is what we risk destroying in ourselves if we seek to destroy that part of our nature, our creativity and passion, our very souls? What do we risk destroying in ourselves when we try to destroy, literally, that metaphorical, that imaginary "other?"

Cecilia Woloch, 2018

Acknowledgements

I would likely never have begun this work, much less seen it through, were it not for the enthusiasm and support of my mentors Eloise Klein Healy, catalyst extraordinaire, and Holly Prado Northup, whose faith and guidance have been priceless jewels.

Nor could I have made the series of journeys during which the poem was first written were it not for the friends who welcomed me, along the way — warmly and repeatedly — into their homes and their lives. I'm especially grateful to Sarah Luczaj and Lukasz Luczaj in the Carpathians; Richard Boulez in Warsaw; Marcin Cienski in Krakow; Dana Nain-Rudovic and Dieter Nain in Berlin; Dagmar Meyer in Basel, Switzerland; Gerald Kurth in Bern; Ursula Perinelli in Lorrach, Germany; Wilfried and Marga Merkel in Rheinfelden; Isabelle Pieri and Pierre Poilloux in Alfortville, France; Adrian Leeds in Paris; Jill Singer in London; Melica Pesic in London; and to the many strangers who came to my rescue when I thought I was lost. During these years, it was my mother's house, in Shepherdsville, Kentucky, that was always the home to which I returned — or rather, it was my mother, herself, who was home. Her spirit and her voice — always singing, always questioning — continue to guide me.

I'm also grateful to Ken Bullock, who accompanied me on my first trip to post-Communist Poland, and to Hawthornden Castle International Retreat for Writers in Midlothian, Scotland, where I was able to work on the manuscript with the River Esk as background music. A debt of gratitude is due, as well, to CEC/Artslink International, for a grant that made possible one of several trips to the Carpathians; to Isabel Fonseca, whose book on the Gypsies, <u>Bury Me Standing</u>, was both an inspiration and a valuable resource; and to the editors of <u>The Roads of the Roma</u> — Ian Hancock, Siobhan Dowd, and Rajko Djuric — for their chronology of Roma history, from which a large part of my own chronological notes have been drawn. The italicized quotations in the Los Angeles section of the poem are taken from a broadcast of the National Public Radio program "Fresh Air," an interview with Chris Hedges, Balkan Bureau Chief for The New York Times, that aired in November of 1997.

    Several sections from the earliest drafts of the poem appeared in the first issue of *The Cider Press Review*, for which I thank the editors, Robert Wynne and Caron Andregg. I am also deeply grateful to the members of Cahuenga Press — Holly Prado-Northup, Harry Northup, James Cushing and Phoebe MacAdams-Ozuna — for first publishing *Tsigan* in book form and for helping usher it out into the world.

    After *Tsigan: The Gypsy Poem* was published in 2001, many other friends and supporters helped to bring it to life and expand its reach and scope. My thanks and love to independent filmmaker Paula Foust, whose efforts made possible the first multi-media presentation of the poem, in April 2013, as part of the University of Southern California's Visions and Voices initiative; thanks, also, to Dr. Stephen Smith, executive director of the Shoah Foundation at USC, to my colleagues at USC, and to the artists who contributed their passion and skill to that performance: stage director Alfredo Avila; musical director/guitarist Ethan Margolis; dancer/choreographer Chitli Ocampo; flamenco vocalist Jose Cortes; filmmaker

Lisa Leeman; film editor Dan Shulman-Means; and poet-performer Andrew Ramirez.

Anastassia Politi, director of la Compagnie Erinna, provided the force and energy that made possible the publication of the French translation of *Tsigan* by Scribe-l'Harmattan in 2014 — which, in turn, would not have been possible without the beautiful rendering of the text into French by Jennifer Bocquentin, who took it on as a labor of love at a difficult moment in her own life. I'm grateful to Osama Khalil, editor at Scribe-l'Harmattan, and to the performers who helped to launch the French edition: Joanne Furlan and the late Konstantinos Graham, whose beautiful voice lives on in recordings of the text of the poem made by Felipe Caramelos. I'm also grateful to Felipe for the opportunity to collaborate with participants in the festival *le Bruit de la Neige* to create an audio performance of the text.

In Poland, the mantle of *Tsigan* was taken up by my friend Maciej Pinkowski, who brought the poem to the attention of the staff at the Museum of the History of Polish Jews (POLIN), which subsequently made possible a bi-lingual performance of *Tsigan* as part of the museum's commemoration of International Holocaust Remembrance Day in 2015. My thanks to the staff at POLIN, to stage director Karolina Kirsz, to Polish actress Ernestyna Winnetka, to musician/composer Paweł Leszczynski, to Agata Wałachowska for film projections and to Jan Piekło, for his Polish translations of the text. I'm also grateful to friend and curator Monika Weychart for including *Tsigan* in the exhibition of Roma art, *Houses as Silver as Tents*.

My gratitude also to Marek Isztok, who first brought *Tsigan* to the attention of the Roma People Foundation in Oswiecim, and to the foundation's chairman, Roman Kwiatkowski, for inviting me to participate in the 2017 Commemoration of the Roma Holocaust at Auschwitz-Birkenau, and for making me feel so welcome in the extended family of the Roma community. I'm indebted to Marek Kazmierski for introducing me to Monika Blaszczak, and to Monika Blaszczak for welcoming me into the fold of *Dikh He Na Bister — Roma Genocide Remembrance*, in the summer of 2017, and for introducing me to the beautiful young people of the International Roma Youth Network.

Dr. Ian Hancock has continued to be a valuable source of both information and inspiration; an interview with him that was broadcast on KPFK radio in December 2014 provided material that helped me to fill in some of the blank spaces in my knowledge of the situation facing the Roma in post-WWII Europe. It was this growing awareness of gaps in my understanding, and the world's, of the history of the Roma people, that led me to want to update and expand the original text of the poem. In this endeavor, the support of friends who have read and re-read and made suggestions about the manuscript have been invaluable — love and thanks, especially, to Sarah Luczaj, Carine Topal and Collin Kelley. The research and encouragement of Paul Polansky have also been important to me. For their encouragement and friendship, I'm also grateful to Hedina Sijercic, Andree Morgan Andrews and Luminita Ciabo; Luminita and the U.S. Embassy in Bucharest made it possible for me to spend several magical days in Sibiu, Romania, in the company of Romani poets and musicians from around the world. Finally, my deepest thanks to Kelli Russell Agodon and Annette Spaulding-Convy of Two Sylvias press for their enthusiasm and dedication to making this new edition of *Tsigan* a reality.

There are many others, too many to name, even to count. This poem has carried me farther than I ever knew I could be carried, and it's always been a collaborative undertaking; somehow, since I began to write it, I've never been alone.

Cecilia Woloch is the author of six previous collections of poems, most recently *Carpathia* (BOA Editions 2009) and *Earth* (Two Sylvias Press 2015), as well as a novel, *Sur la Route* (Quale Press 2015). *Tsigan: The Gypsy Poem*, originally published by Cahuenga Press in 2001, has been adapted for multi-media performances around the world, was published in French translation by Scribe l'Harmattan in 2014, and has been updated and expanded for a new English edition from Two Sylvias Press. In addition to French, Cecilia's work has also been translated into German, Bulgarian, Hungarian, Polish, Romanes and Ukrainian. Her awards include a fellowship from the National Endowment for the Arts, a Pushcart Prize, *The Indiana Review* Poetry Prize, *The New Ohio Review* Poetry Prize, and residencies around the world. Currently based in Los Angeles, she spends half of the year on the road.

Publications by Two Sylvias Press:

*The Daily Poet: Day-By-Day Prompts
For Your Writing Practice*
by Kelli Russell Agodon and Martha Silano (Print and eBook)

The Daily Poet Companion Journal (Print)

*Fire On Her Tongue:
An Anthology of Contemporary Women's Poetry*
edited by Kelli Russell Agodon and Annette Spaulding-Convy
(Print and eBook)

The Poet Tarot and Guidebook: A Deck Of Creative Exploration
(Print)

Tsigan
by Cecilia Woloch (Print and eBook)

PR for Poets
by Jeannine Hall Gailey (Print and eBook)

Appalachians Run Amok,
Winner of the 2016 Two Sylvias Press Wilder Prize
by Adrian Blevins (Print and eBook)

Killing Marias
by Claudia Castro Luna (Print and eBook)

The Ego and the Empiricist,
Finalist 2016 Two Sylvias Press Chapbook Prize
by Derek Mong (Print and eBook)

The Authenticity Experiment
by Kate Carroll de Gutes (Print and eBook)

Mytheria, Finalist 2015 Two Sylvias Press Wilder Prize
by Molly Tenenbaum (Print and eBook)

Arab in Newsland ,
Winner of the 2016 Two Sylvias Press Chapbook Prize
by Lena Khalaf Tuffaha (Print and eBook)

The Blue Black Wet of Wood,
Winner of the 2015 Two Sylvias Press Wilder Prize
by Carmen R. Gillespie (Print and eBook)

Fire Girl: Essays on India, America, and the In-Between
by Sayantani Dasgupta (Print and eBook)

Blood Song
by Michael Schmeltzer (Print and eBook)

Naming The No-Name Woman,
Winner of the 2015 Two Sylvias Press Chapbook Prize
by Jasmine An (Print and eBook)

Community Chest
by Natalie Serber (Print)

Phantom Son: A Mother's Story of Surrender
by Sharon Estill Taylor (Print and eBook)

What The Truth Tastes Like
by Martha Silano (Print and eBook)

landscape/heartbreak
by Michelle Peñaloza (Print and eBook)

Earth, Winner of the 2014 Two Sylvias Press Chapbook Prize
by Cecilia Woloch (Print and eBook)

The Cardiologist's Daughter
by Natasha Kochicheril Moni (Print and eBook)

She Returns to the Floating World
by Jeannine Hall Gailey (Print and eBook)

Hourglass Museum
by Kelli Russell Agodon (eBook)

Cloud Pharmacy
by Susan Rich (eBook)

Dear Alzheimer's: A Caregiver's Diary & Poems
by Esther Altshul Helfgott (eBook)

Listening to Mozart: Poems of Alzheimer's
by Esther Altshul Helfgott (eBook)

*Crab Creek Review 30th Anniversary Issue
featuring Northwest Poets*
edited by Kelli Russell Agodon and Annette Spaulding-Convy
(eBook)